Boffin Boy
Set Three
Workbook One

By David Orme

Accompanies the Boffin Boy reading books

- Boffin Boy Goes to Hollywood
- Boffin Boy and the Poison Garden
- Boffin Boy and the Lost Yeti

Ransom

Boffin Boy Set Three Workbook One
by David Orme

Illustrated by Peter Richardson

Published by Ransom Publishing Ltd.
Radley House, 8 St. Cross Road, Winchester, Hampshire SO23 9HX, UK
www.ransom.co.uk

ISBN   978 178127 052 3
First published in 2013

Design and layout: RedPaperDesign.co.uk

Find out more about Boffin Boy at
www.ransom.co.uk

CONTENTS

INTRODUCTION

The purpose of this material is to provide opportunities to check student's understanding of the Boffin Boy stories and to provide structures to encourage writing in a range of forms.

Students working at the reading level assumed by these books frequently have a mis-match between their experiential oral skills and their skills in reading and writing. The Boffin Boy stories and support materials are intended to be:

- appealing and engaging, particularly to those who may be otherwise reluctant to read, but appropriate as a fun read for all students;

- highly visual, with minimum text in the stories and minimum rubric on the worksheets;

- age appropriate;

- achievable; and

- appropriately challenging.

This Workbook covers three of the Boffin Boy titles: *Boffin Boy Goes to Hollywood*, *Poison Garden* and *The Lost Yeti*. There are eight worksheets for each title, plus two sheets of artwork resources that students can use in various ways, including designing their own Boffin Boy graphic novels. Further ideas for these are provided in the teacher's notes. The Boffin Boy Set One and Set Two workbooks contain additional artwork resources.

The worksheets have a literacy focus, but include a range of lighter, fun activities such as word searches and code-breaking. The sheets are introduced by a character from the story and, in keeping with the stories, are slightly more wacky and offbeat than the traditional literacy worksheet!

Each sheet is fully supported by teacher's notes. For these students it is essential that the work on the sheets is prepared as a class or group exercise, and suggestions for this are provided (suggestions include oral work and shared writing). Simply handing out the sheets, perhaps as a homework exercise, is unlikely to be successful.

Worksheet 1 – Boffin Boy's Brainy Quiz

Task:

This a straightforward comprehension exercise with multiple-choice answers.

Support:

Discuss the events of the story with the students before starting the exercise. Note that the questions are given in the same sequence as the events in the story.

The final question requires the students to suggest appropriate answers.

Extension:

Construct a multiple-choice activity based on one of the other Boffin Boy books in this series.

Worksheet 2 – TV Report

Task:

To complete the sentences on the worksheet to produce a news report.

Support:

This is a retelling of part of the story. The students are asked to complete the sentences from the viewpoint of the two newsreaders.

If appropriate, the students could be encouraged to fill in the gaps with more detail; possibly by looking at the pictures for additional information.

Extension:

Develop the news report into a drama activity and ask the students to work in pairs to present this to the rest of the group.

Worksheet 3 – Face and Hands

Task:

To explore gesture and expression as a means of communication.

Support:

Discuss with the students how it is possible to tell what people are thinking or feeling from their facial expressions. If appropriate, make reference to emoticons and discuss why people use these in electronic communication. Why do we need artificial indicators if we cannot see people's faces or hear their voices?

Look at the examples of the hand gestures and facial expressions on the worksheet. Identify what the characters are thinking and feeling. The students are asked to provide a written interpretation for each one.

Extension:

Ask the students to work in pairs to extend the work on expressions and gestures. One student should act as a model while the other draws.

Alternatively, ask the students to collect examples of such symbols that they have found on social media etc., to draw them and explain what they mean.

Worksheet 4 – Design a Superhero

Task:

A drawing activity: to develop the idea of a superhero.

Support:

Discuss why the superheroes in the story are useless. Note that in many cases the names given to the superheroes might indicate this.

Ask the students to decide whether they are going to design a brilliant superhero or a useless one.

The students then need to think about the attributes their hero will have. Discuss what qualities a superhero would be expected to have. List these on the board if necessary.

Note that superheroes may have several good qualities (e.g. honesty, kind to animals and small children, etc.) and also in some cases they may have more than one super power. Other heroes may not have super powers but, like Boffin Boy, rely on their intelligence (and a sidekick).

It may be a good idea to leave the naming of their superhero until they have completed the rest of the exercise.

Extension:

All the best superheroes have one or more special enemies. Ask the students to design and describe their superhero's enemy.

This could be another drawing activity or could be done as a piece of writing.

Worksheet 5 – Excuses!

Task:

To suggest inappropriate excuses for the superheroes.

Support:

Note that the superheroes clearly do not want to go and help Colonel Bullet. Review with the students the excuses put forward by the superheroes in the story and identify why these are inappropriate.

The students are required to provide on the worksheet another inappropriate excuse for each of the characters.

Extension:

Ask the students to work together in small groups to create a booklet of excuses. This could be 'Excuses for not doing homework', 'Excuses for getting home late', 'Excuses for having a messy bedroom' – or the students could suggest their own.

This could be an ICT opportunity.

Worksheet 6 – The Wizard of Edo's Secret Diary

Task:

To write in the first person. To write from another character's point of view.

Support:

Review the story with the students, from the point of view of the Wizard of Edo.

The students are asked to complete the Wizard of Edo's diary on the worksheet. Note that the events will be interpreted by the Wizard as they affect his plans.

The students can complete the sheet in short sentences, but they could also provide a little more detail about the Wizard's feelings as the story progresses.

Extension:

Ask the students to write the Wizard of Edo's diary for the previous week. This should start:

'I've just had this really brilliant idea. ... '

Before attempting this task the students should re-read the story, to ensure that they know what the Wizard wants.

They should be encouraged to provide details of his plans in his diary entries.

Worksheet 7 – The Super Rat

Task:

To identify the features of a super rat and to label a diagram.

Support:

Work through the labelled features of the rat with the students. Discuss what each feature would enable the super rat to do. If appropriate, read with the students the section of the story relating to the rats.

Note that the students are asked to find appropriate adjectives for the claws and eyes. Encourage them to suggest interesting words for these. Ensure that they understand the word 'vicious'.

Discuss whether there might be any other features the super rat may have. If so, add labels for these features.

The final part of the task is to write a story plan. Refer to the task in Boffin Boy and the Lost Yeti, Worksheet 6, to find a model for this. Alternatively, provide the students with prompts which are specific to this story.

Extension:

Ask the students to write part of the story about the escaped rat, based on their story plan.

Worksheet 8 – My Favourite Character

Task:

To produce a social media page for a chosen character.

Support:

This worksheet is open-ended and may be used to support any of the Boffin Boy reading books.

The students are required to decide which is their favourite 'Boffin Boy' character and to give their reasons for this.

They are then asked to create a social media ('Facemate') page for their character.

Discuss with the students what sort of information is usually given on a social media site. The students will need to decide:

- their character's friends
- places the character has visited
- pets the character has
- other likes and dislikes
- any other details, e.g. enemies.

Some of this information can be obtained from the stories; some will need to be made up.

Encourage the students to be creative in their writing.

Extension:

This could be an ICT activity, with the students creating their page on the computer.

Can you find the right answer?
And the prize is – er, sorry, there
isn't one.

1. Why was I cross at the start of the story?
A   Green Tights Man woke me up.
B   Green Tights Man is a better superhero than me.
C   I wasn't invited.
D   Green Tights Man has a better costume than me.

2. The superheroes didn't want to help Colonel Bullet! Why not?
A   They didn't want to interrupt the show because they might get an award.
B   They were too scared.
C   They were too busy.
D   They didn't like Colonel Bullet very much.

3. What did Colonel Bullet want them to do?
A   Capture the Wizard of Edo.
B   Find where the Wizard of Edo lives.
C   Capture the giant rats.
D   Appear on live TV.

4. What happened to the superheroes when they got to the Wizard's hideout?
A   They started planning their next move.
B   They found a way to get inside.
C   The idiots all got captured.
D   They found the Wizard of Edo.

5. What did I decide to do?
A   Go and sort it out.
B   Ring up Wu Pee and ask him what to do.
C   Send Wu Pee to sort it out.
D   Try and become superhero of the year.

6. What did the Wizard of Edo want?
A   To take over the world.
B   To release the giant rats.
C   To defeat the superheroes.
D   His own TV series.

7. How was the wizard defeated?
A   Katt the dog called in his friends.
B   The superheroes escaped.
C   The rats escaped and frightened the wizard.
D   I sorted it out.

8. What happened at the awards ceremony?
(You need to think of the right answer and three wrong ones.)
A   _____
B   _____
C   _____
D   _____

Can you finish this news report? It's all about me!

There were amazing scenes at the .... today.

The world's greatest superheroes were

....

Suddenly, ... arrived and told them ....

All the superheroes

....

They couldn't escape because

....

The brave superheroes agreed to do it when

....

Sometimes hands and faces are as good as words when we want to tell people something. What are these characters saying?

_____

_____

_____

_____

_____

_____

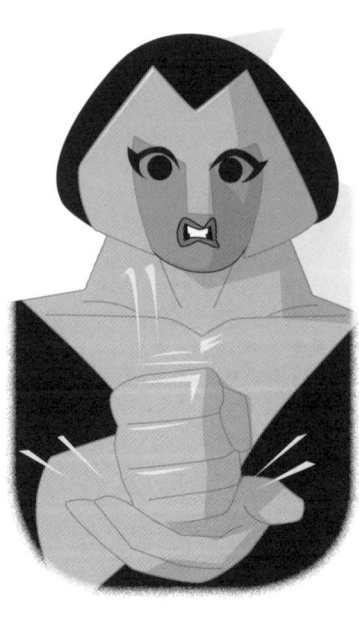

_____

_____

_____

_____

The superheroes in this story are all useless! (Apart from Boffin Boy and me, of course.)

Design your own superhero!

My superhero is brilliant ☐ useless ☐ .

Name: _____

Costume: _____

What they are good at:
_____

What they are bad at:
_____

What prize they might have
won at the award ceremony:
_____

11

Fill in the gaps in my diary – or else!

I nearly got what I really, really wanted – but then my plan went wrong!

First, Colonel Bullet _____

Luckily, they were all useless and I _____

_____

_____

But then _____ and _____ turned up. I really

hate _____ !

They defeated me by _____

_____

_____

_____

Just you wait! I'll be back!

My super rats were great!

_____ eyes, so it can
_____

Clever brain, so it can
_____

Huge tummy, so it can
_____

_____ teeth, to
_____

Vicious claws, so it can _____

One of the rats has escaped! What did it do? Write a story plan.

_____

_____

_____

_____

_____

_____

_____

_____

_____

_____

14

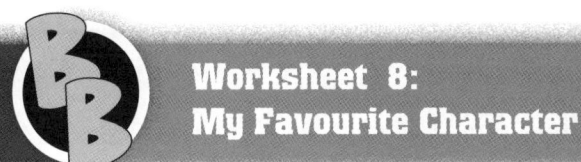

Who's your favourite character?
Hope it's me!

My favourite character is _____

I like this character because _____

_____

Write a Facemate page for your character.

Friends

Places visited

Pets

Likes and dislikes

More about me

Worksheet 1 – How to Turn Someone into a Tree

Task:

To write instructions.

Support:

Review with the students the section of the story in which Daffney tries to turn Boffin Boy and Polly into trees. Then work through the list of instructions on the worksheet.

Discuss with the students why eating apples wouldn't work on a dog. Ask for suggestions to identify foodstuffs a dog might eat.

The remaining instructions on the list can be completed just by reference to the story.

The final part of the activity asks the students to explain how Boffin Boy turns the trees back into their original form. This can be a simple one sentence answer – for example, he invents a potion and waters the trees with it – or it could be a more complex answer. It will be best to discuss various possibilities with the students if you require a longer answer.

Extension:

Ask the students to write a set of instructions. This could be for something relevant to the story, or it could be a simple list of instructions related to everyday life.

To extend the activity still further, the students could be asked to turn these into an instruction leaflet.

The students could choose their own subject, but it may be more appropriate to give them a list of suggestions.

Worksheet 2 – Daffney's Maze

Task:

To decode the list of ingredients for Daffney's potion.

Support:

The first part of the task is for the students to find the correct route through the maze. As they move along the correct path through the maze, the students should note the letters and numbers they pass. They will always meet a letter followed by a number.

Each item on the ingredients list can then be identified from these letter/number pairs, using the key provided.

The complete recipe is as follows:

f 6	a puddle of	rain from the desert
d 4	a squirt of	octopus juice
i 9	two strings of	spider web
l 12	three drips of	dinosaur blood
b 2	a mash of	strawberry jellyfish
n 14	a splurt of	dragon sweat
c 3	one	hair from a dog
p 15	a scrape of	powdered silver
h 8	five	apple pips
k 11	a	nice cup of tea.

The second part of the task is to write out the potion in full. A sentence starter is provided on the sheet. The students should write out the potion in full on a separate sheet.

Extension:

Ask the students to identify the unused ingredients. They should write this list out and suggest what this potion could make.

The students could write further potion lists for other things that Daffney may like to turn her victims into. These lists could use some of the ingredients given, or the students could use their own ideas.

Worksheet 3 – Wu Pee Wants to Know!

Task:

To retell the story using conversation.

Support

Ensure that the students understand that, in answering Wu Pee's questions, Polly and Boffin Boy are explaining the events of the story to Wu Pee. If appropriate, review the story before starting this worksheet.

The answers to Wu Pee's questions can all be found in the text. For the final part of the worksheet, the students are asked to devise a further question and to provide an answer. This could be slightly more challenging.

Alternatively, the students could write the question and then give it to a friend to answer.

Extension:

Ask the students to use the completed worksheet to help them write a conversation between Polly and Wu Pee using direct speech. This could be a continuation of the phone conversation using the question and answer style, or it could be an explanation of how Polly felt during the adventure.

Worksheet 4 – Danger – Daffney!

Task:

To write a description and character sketch of Daffney.

Support:

Ask the students to look at the picture of Daffney on the worksheet. Discuss her physical characteristics. Discuss the best way of warning people about her actions.

Note that the information on the worksheet is to be presented on a web site, so it will need to be quite brief and punchy.

Note that Daffney may try to disguise herself.

Discuss with the students what is the best thing to do and not to do if you meet Daffney. Add these ideas to the worksheet.

Extension:

Ask the students to use the completed sheet to design a web page warning about Daffney. This could be an ICT activity, with students creating a web page on the computer.

Alternatively, the students could use the model to create a web page warning about a cartoon villain of their choice.

Worksheet 5 – Picture Brief

Task:

To write a picture brief.

Support:

Locate the picture on the worksheet in the story. Ensure that the students understand the purpose of a picture brief. Discuss with the students what information will be needed for the illustrator.

Stress the importance of facial expressions. What is Katt thinking and how does his face show this? How does the character's posture help move the story along?

For the second task the picture brief could be completed as a class/group activity.

Extension:

Ask the students to think about a new scene for the end of the story, where Daffney outgrows her pot and escapes. The students should then write a picture brief for this scene. It may or may not include any of the other characters.

The students could then pass on their brief to a friend to illustrate.

Worksheet 6 – A Letter from the Council

Task:

To write a formal letter.

Support:

Discuss with the students the layout of the letter on the worksheet. What should go in the space on the left of the sheet, under 'Dr Daffney'?

The students should make up an address for her; this address could be based on what the students know about her house e.g. Big Tree Lane, Sun Block Road, Next door to Polly.

Discuss what issues the neighbours might have – e.g. the speed with which things grow, strange noises when dogs are captured, the disappearance of visitors (the post person, the

double-glazing salesman, the paper boy/girl), etc.

Discuss what action the council might want Dr Daffney to take, and what they might threaten to do if she takes no action.

Extension:

Ask the students to draft a letter to the council, as a reply from Daffney. She might simply tell the council she's not going to comply, or she might invite Mr. Bigboss round for tea!

Worksheet 7 – Story Quiz

Task:

A straightforward comprehension exercise.

Support:

Explain to the students that the answers to all of the questions on the worksheet can be found by reading through the story. The questions are sequential.

The students could write short answers, or they could be asked to write in full sentences, as appropriate.

Extension:

Ask the students to use this story quiz worksheet as a model to write a similar sheet of questions for one of the other Boffin Boy stories in the series.

Worksheet 8 – Dr Daffney's Trees

Task:

A drawing activity.

Support:

With the students, look at the trees shown in the story. Discuss how the trees have been made to look like the characters named.

The task is to draw four trees on the worksheet. The first three trees on the sheet are labelled and the students are asked to create features on these trees to indicate what they are.

The dog tree can be modelled on pictures from the book; a pop star tree can be given specific features or simply indicated by a microphone, musical instrument, etc. The footballer tree could be given features or club colours.

The final tree is left blank for students to create their own idea. It may be appropriate to list suggestions from the class before the students begin the task.

Extension:

Ask the students to write a 'How to care for your … tree' sheet.

Make a list of care and information points, such as what to feed your tree, how big it grows, what conditions it likes (sun/shade), and any warnings. When the list is complete, use it to create the leaflet.

Worksheet 1: How to Turn Someone into a Tree

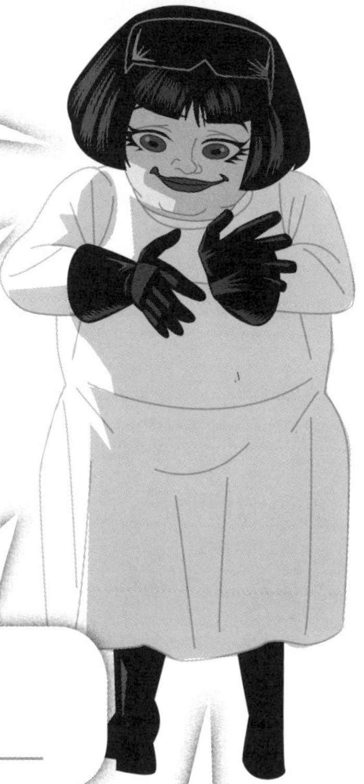

This is how I did it! Clever, eh!

1. Catch your person. The best way is to make them fall asleep by

____

____

2. This won't work for a dog! The best way for them is

____

3. Bring the person or dog to

____

4. Turn them into a tree by

____

5. Plant them in the garden.

Boffin Boy finds a way to turn the trees back into people and dogs! How does he do it?

____

____

____

____

This is really a-MAZE-ing!

Follow the maze to find my secret garden. On the way you might discover my potion recipe!

WAY IN

SECRET GARDEN

1) ham sandwiches
2) strawberry jellyfish
3) hair from a dog (to give the tree its bark)
4) octopus juice
5) sausage rolls
6) rain from the desert
7) cow pats
8) apple pips
9) spider web
10) chocolate cake
11) nice cup of tea
12) dinosaur blood
13) earwig eyes
14) dragon sweat
15) powdered silver

a) thirty
b) a mash of
c) one
d) a squirt of
e) four mouldy
f) a puddle of
g) five large
h) five
i) two strings of
j) a squidgy
k) a
l) three drips of
m) eight
n) a splurt of
p) a scrape of

Now write out Daffney's potion:

Mix the ingredients together, then _____

_____

_____

What was strange about those trees?

_____

So why did you go into her garden?

_____

So why did you eat those apples?

_____

How did you manage to get out of that cage?

_____

What did you do to her when you caught her?

_____

Why did she want to turn dogs and people into trees?

_____

Can you think of another question Wu Pee might have asked?

Wu Pee: _____

Answer: _____

I put up a warning about Daffney on my website – wupeethewizard.com.
Can you help me finish it?

WARNING

Name:

What she looks like:

What she will do to you:

How to keep safe:

In this picture I came to the rescue! Write a picture brief for the illustrator.

_____

_____

_____

_____

_____

_____

_____

_____

There was going to be a picture of Daffney mixing up her potion in the book, but there wasn't room! Can you draw the picture and write a brief?

_____

_____

_____

_____

_____

_____

I complained about those trees!
Finish this letter the council sent
to Daffney.

ARCADIA BOROUGH COUNCIL
Council Offices, High Street, Arcadia

Dr Daffney

. . . .

. . . .

. . . .

Dear Doctor Daffney,
Your neighbours are complaining about your garden. They say that ....

....

....

....

Will you please

....

....

....

If you don't, we will

....

....

....

Yours sincerely
T.H.E. Bigboss (Town Clerk)

Warning! Too many wrong answers and I'll be after you!

What made Polly cross at the start of the story?

....

Why was Boffin Boy worried when Katt went through the hedge?

....

How did Polly and Boffin Boy get into Daffney's garden?

....

What shouldn't they have done in the garden?

....

How did Daffney turn dogs and people into trees?

....

What made Daffney run away?

....

At the end of the story Daffney thought 'Get that creature off me!' What was she worried about?

....

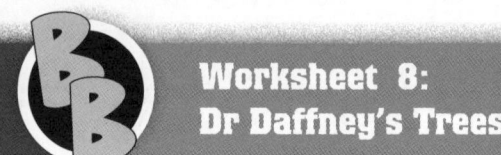

Those trees have got to go!

Daffney decides to sell her trees online. Think of a name for her website. Draw the trees, then write a description of each one.

Website name _____

Dog tree

_____

_____

Pop star tree

_____

_____

Footballer tree

_____

_____

_____

_____

Worksheet 1 – All Mixed Up

Task:

A sequencing activity – telling the story.

Support:

This is a straightforward activity. The students are asked to retell the story by putting the sentences on the worksheet in the correct order.

If necessary, review the story with the students before they start the exercise. They could begin by numbering the sentences, before writing them into the spaces on the worksheet.

Note that the final sentence at the end of the story should indicate that our heroes return to the present – but arrive on Mount Everest.

Extension:

Ask the students to write some more sentences to extend the story. The number of sentences required should reflect the student's own level of competence.

Note that the story ends with the heroes arriving, not where they had left, but stranded at the top of Everest.

Discuss the various possibilities for our heroes to reach home – e.g. the mobile phones work, Boffin Boy's spaceman friend rescues them, they are found by a party of climbers, etc.

Worksheet 2 – Newspaper Report

Task:

To write a newspaper report about the yeti sighting.

Support:

The students are asked to write a newspaper report about the sighting of the yeti. Note that the newspaper report is not written by, or about, Boffin Boy. The only reference to Boffin Boy is the picture credit.

Ask the students to imagine that they are the person (or people) who saw the yeti, and that the report is based on their story.

Discuss what the conditions were like on the top of the mountain when Boffin Boy saw the yeti – e.g. crowded, snowy, misty. Ask the students to decide what information should go into the article.

Discuss whether a description of the yeti is needed. It may not be needed, as most people know what a yeti is supposed to look like. Discuss how the people seeing the yeti might have reacted. How might the yeti have reacted to the people?

Make notes with the group to provide a logical structure for the article, then ask the students to complete the front page.

Extension:

A different strange creature turns up outside the school!

Ask the students to write the newspaper story covering this event.

Worksheet 3 – Imaginary Creatures

Task:

To create an imaginary creature. Drawing and writing.

Support:

Discuss with the students the yeti as portrayed in the story. Note that many people have heard of the yeti and would probably be able to describe it if asked.

Ask the students to give examples of other imaginary creatures they have heard of – e.g. a unicorn, the Loch Ness Monster, Big Foot, dragon. Ask the students to try to describe one of these orally.

Ask the students to suggest types of imaginary creatures of their own. If the students have read any other Boffin Boy books, they could give examples of imaginary creatures from those books. List these suggestions on the board.

Choose one of the suggestions to model a written description. Sketch the creature and then discuss how to begin the description. Ask what features are not shown in the picture – e.g.

colour, relative size, whether it has bad breath. Note these on the board.

If appropriate, continue to model the written description.

Extension:

This could be an ICT opportunity. Ask the students to research some of the imaginary creatures listed and discussed in the first part of the activity. If appropriate, they could also search for other imaginary creatures.

The students could print out appropriate information and pictures for display.

Worksheet 4 – Messages on the Rock

Task:

To complete the warning messages Boffin Boy left on the big rock.

Support:

This is a straightforward activity. If appropriate, discuss with the students possible endings for the messages before completing the worksheet.

There is a space for the students to make up their own message or messages.

Extension:

Ask the students to draw the rock from the other side – i.e. from the 'yeti' side. Ask them to put messages from the yeti onto the rock. These messages could be taken from the text in the book, or they could be taken from Worksheet 5, which focuses on the yeti 'language'. Alternatively the students could draw yeti warning signs, instead of writing.

Worksheet 5 – The Yeti Language

Task:

To undertake a careful reading of the text.

Support:

The worksheet shows a number of expressions in the yeti 'language', which the students

are required to translate, using the story as a source.

Identify the pages in the book which show the yeti words and their translations. Note that these occur on more than one page.

The 'answers' are:

Yiggy yoggy blib	It's those funny creatures again.
Bloppy ding	Good job I've got my camera.
Ploppy glimp	Grab them.
Swiggle neep	Your turn next.
Snoppy gloop	Our new god is angry.

Note that the yeti 'language' is entirely nonsense and that the students should not try to find a direct match between the 'words'. This is important for the final section of the worksheet, where the students are asked to 'translate' a sentence which needs them to invent some 'words' for themselves.

Extension:

Take the idea of translation a stage further and ask the students to create a phrase book for Boffin Boy and Wu Pee to take on holiday to the yeti world. This should be a selection of words and phrases that might be useful on holiday. e.g. 'A large ice cream please', 'Where is the beach?', etc.

Worksheet 6 – Time Gates

Task:

To develop a story plan.

Support:

Explain to the students how a story plan can help to write the story. Read through the worksheet with the students and ask for suggestions for answers to the questions. Note these on the board if appropriate.

Point out that each student will have different ideas, and they should use and develop these ideas individually as they work through the worksheet.

Extension:

Ask the students to use the story plan to write their own time gate story.

Worksheet 7 – The Yeti's Story

Task:

To write from a different point of view.

Support:

Point out to the students that, in the story, the yetis were probably just as surprised to see Boffin Boy and Wu Pee as *they* were to see the yetis.

As part of this activity the students should draw a picture of the photograph that the yeti took. They can then complete the yeti's description.

Note: the yetis are describing Boffin Boy and Wu Pee, and they will find them very odd. Discuss the features that the yeti might find strange: no hair, clothes, weedy appearance, and so on.

Extension:

Ask the students to write a conversation between the same two yetis, after Boffin Boy and Wu Pee escape at the end of the story.

Worksheet 8 – An Extra Section

Task:

To write an extra paragraph for the story.

Support:

This is an imaginative piece of writing. It is to be written from Katt's point of view.

Ensure that the students appreciate that Katt remained unseen until he chose to reveal himself. Note that, at the end of the story, Katt is revealed to have the power to transform himself into a much more threatening creature. Would this have been one of the reasons why he is accepted as their god?

Discuss other abilities and attributes that might have persuaded the yetis to make him a god. List these on the board if appropriate. The students could also include details about how he was treated – put on the throne, given lots of cups of tea, etc.

Extension:

Use the paragraph the students have written as a basis for a graphic novel-style continuation of the text.

The students could draw the necessary scenes, or could use the photocopiable section at the back of this workbook.

Alternatively this could be an ICT opportunity and the work could be created on the computer.

I'm in a muddle as usual! Can you put these sentences in the right order?

☐ Wu Pee and Boffin Boy are about to be sacrificed.

☐ As usual, they are saved by Katt.

☐ They go back through the time gate.

☐ Boffin Boy, Wu Pee and Katt go back to Scotland. They follow the yeti.

☐ Boffin Boy and Katt go mountain climbing in Scotland.

☐ They are captured by the yetis.

☐ Katt has become the yeti's new god.

☐ They see a yeti in the mist.

The last sentence is missing! What happens at the end of the story?

9 ....

I sent my picture to the Mountain Times! Can you write the story to go with it?

MOUNTAIN TIMES

MONSTERS SEEN ON MOUNTAIN!

Is this the yeti?
Credit: photo taken by Boffin Boy.

Today on Mount ....
climbers reported that ....

....

....

....

....

....

....

....

....

....

....

Name of creature ....

Description of your creature: ....
....
....

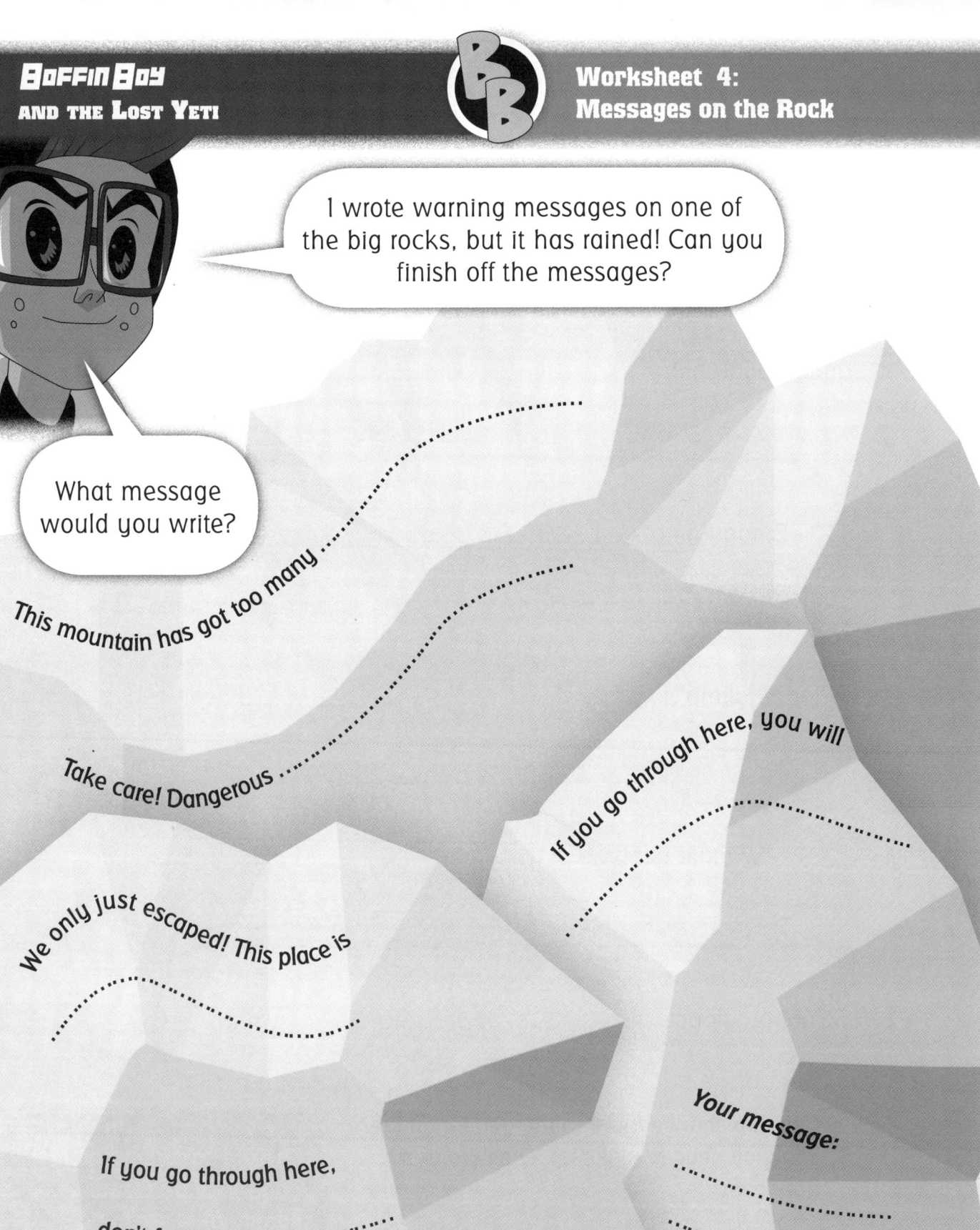

I wrote warning messages on one of the big rocks, but it has rained! Can you finish off the messages?

What message would you write?

This mountain has got too many ....

Take care! Dangerous ....

If you go through here, you will ....

We only just escaped! This place is ....

If you go through here, don't forget your ....

Your message: ....

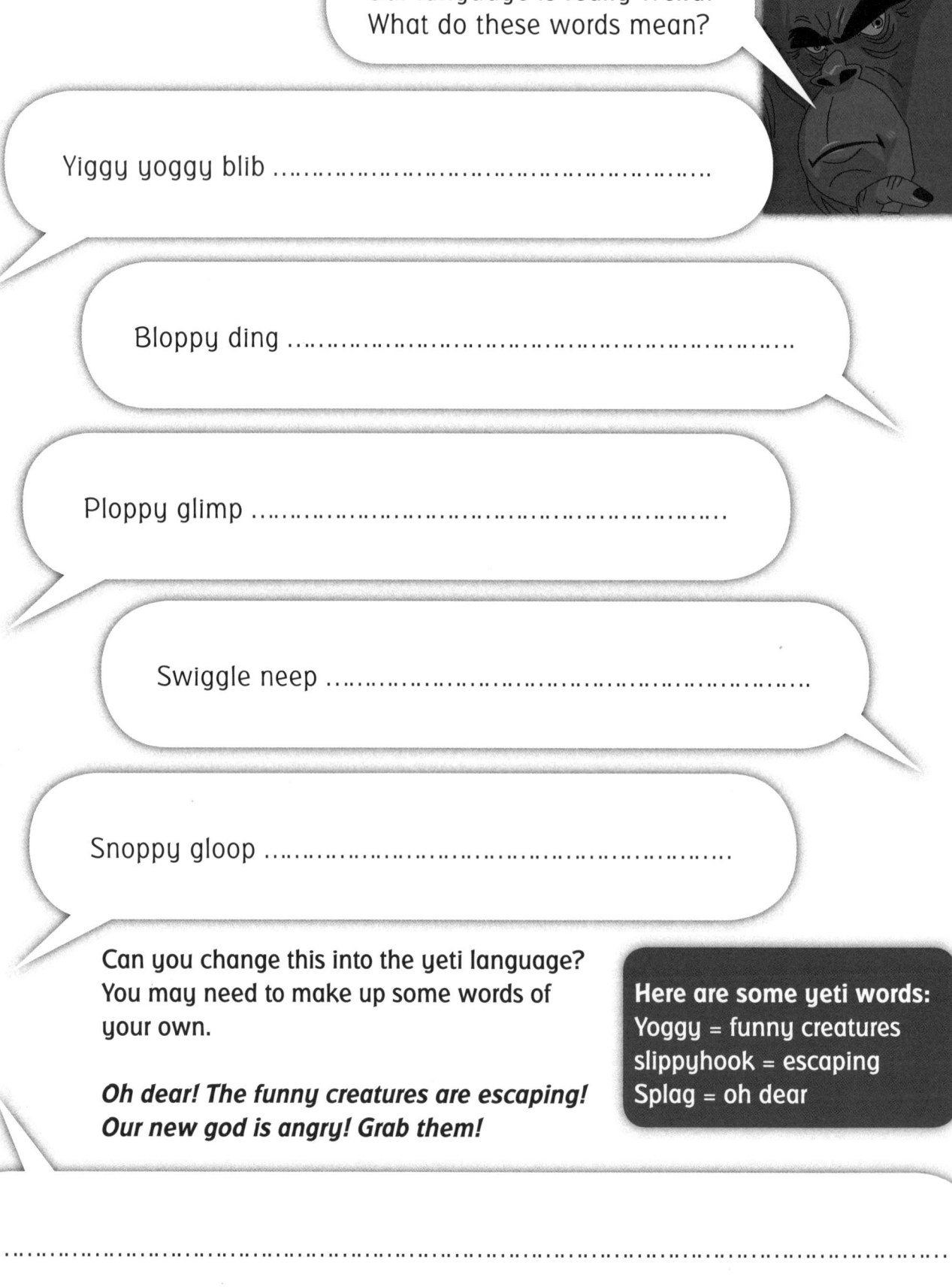

Our language is really weird! What do these words mean?

Yiggy yoggy blib ……………………………………………………

Bloppy ding ……………………………………………………………

Ploppy glimp ………………………………………………………

Swiggle neep …………………………………………………………

Snoppy gloop ………………………………………………………

Can you change this into the yeti language? You may need to make up some words of your own.

Oh dear! The funny creatures are escaping! Our new god is angry! Grab them!

Here are some yeti words:
Yoggy = funny creatures
slippyhook = escaping
Splag = oh dear

……………………………………………………………………………………………………

A time gate lets you travel into the future or the past. Time gates make great stories! Have a go!

Story plan

I will travel into the future/the past.

Where did you find the time gate?

....

Did you travel into the past or the future?

....

Who went with you?

....

....

What happened when you were there?

....

....

....

How did you manage to get back?

....

....

....

In the story I took a photograph of Boffin Boy and Katt. Then I went and told my friends what I saw. What did I tell them?

You'll never believe what I've just seen!

What?

Look at this photo! They were ....

....

....

....

That small creature looks like one of our gods! We'd better

....

....

....

I wasn't captured by the yetis. When Boffin Boy and Wu Pee saw me next, I had become the yeti's new god!

How do you think this happened?

The yetis didn't see me because I hid behind a rock. I followed them to their cave. Then

_____

_____

_____

_____

_____

_____

_____

_____

_____

_____

_____

_____

_____

_____

_____

_____

_____

_____

_____

The following two picture resource pages are provided to enable students to undertake a variety of tasks in a more creative way. More picture resources, including callouts and objects, will be found in the Boffin Boy Set One and Two workbooks.

The following are merely some starting point suggestions for their use:

1. Cut out appropriate pictures of the villains. Create 'Wanted Posters'.

2. Design appropriate backgrounds for one of the stories from the books, or for a new story. Then cut out appropriate characters to illustrate a scene from the book or story.

3. Use the characters, objects and speech / thought bubbles to mock up a page using the graphic novel style.

4. Discuss possible alternative endings for stories, and continue the story in graphic novel format.

5. Develop a board game based on one of the books. Use the characters to produce cards. Create further cards to illustrate weapons.

6. Create puzzles in the same styles as those in the workbooks – word searches, codes, etc.

7. Devise maps for various locations described in the books. Illustrate with appropriate characters.

8. Use as illustrations for pupils' own stories.

9. Design web pages, perhaps by scanning the images and using them in an appropriate design program.

Graphic Novels and ICT

Microsoft Word provides facilities for pupils to design their own graphic novel pages. Objects such as clip art or pupils' own scanned pictures can be imported into the page.

A range of callouts (speech and thought bubbles) are included in Microsoft Word, and can be pasted in. To find them, open the Drawing toolbar, click on Autoshapes then Callouts. Text can then be placed in the callouts, which can be dragged into position.

In addition, the Drawing toolbar offers a Word Art feature ideal for 'sound effect' words such as 'Kaboom!' Text boxes can be used for caption boxes in the pages, and both text boxes and the callouts can have colour fills.